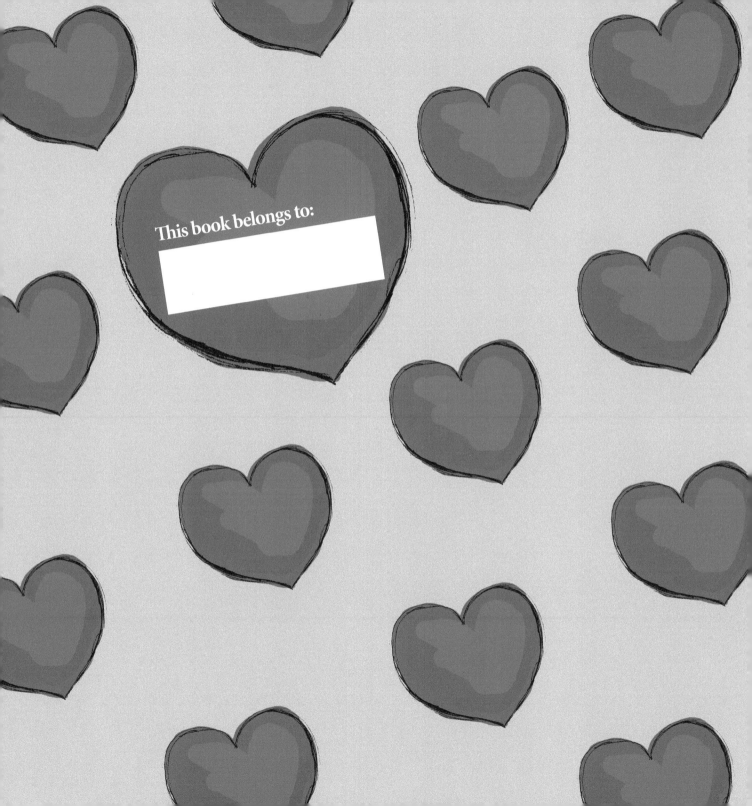

This book belongs to:

¡Bienvenidos a mi mundo! My name is Lulu and this is my family - my Mom and my *Abuelita*.

While my Mom was at work, my *Abuelita* and I would spend a lot of time together as she would take care of me.

My *Abuelita* would share stories about her heritage and customs from her homeland, Puerto Rico. From her, I learned how to speak Spanish.

The sounds of music and the aroma of food filled the house. The meals were so delicious! I used to love to watch my *Abuelita* as she would prepare and cook our meals. As I became older, she taught me how to cook.

I remember her telling me how important it is to keep these traditions in families.

In all the time I spent with my *Abuelita*, the most important lesson I learned was how to love.

te quiero
mucho

She also took care of other children whose Moms were at work. Watching my *Abuelita* with these children taught me so much about patience and caring for others.

Sometimes, I would help my *Abuelita* with the babies – feeding them, changing their diapers and playing with them. I loved hearing the giggles and laughter at playtime.

Recently, there have been changes and things are not the same.

My *Abuelita* is much older now and is no longer able to do things for herself. She now lives at a home with other *Abuelitos* who need help with care and every day activities.

My *Abuelita* struggles to remember the most basic things and many times, will not recognize me anymore. It makes me sad because she is so special to me.

Our visits and my time with her now are so different from how they used to be. Because of these changes, we're not able to talk and do things like we used to.

I was thinking to myself...

What can I do during my visits with my *Abuelita* to show her how much I love her?

What can I do to help her understand?

Then it came to me. I remembered all the things we used to do together and how special and loved it made me feel.

It gave me ideas of how to spend time with her.

Now when we visit, we play music for her and she'll tap her feet on the floor to the sound of the beats.

We bring her favorite foods. I see a smile come upon her as she tastes and savors some of the same foods she would so lovingly prepare for us.

We show her pictures of family, color
in coloring books and decorate
cookies together.

Many days, things can seem confusing for *Abuelita*.

Doing activities with her that are familiar helps to remind her of how she showed us love so many years ago.

As she is able to recollect these memories, her face lights up and I know in that moment she is happy.

I enjoy being able to spend this time with my *Abuelita* and I look forward to our visits. My *Abuelita* may no longer be able to speak or understand things as she used to, but I'm happy there are many other ways to show my *Abuelita* love in what we see, hear and feel as we do things together.

My *Abuelita* is very special and I'm so happy there are many ways I can show her how much I love her.

Color Me

Now it's your turn...

What are some ways in which you can express love?

What are your favorite songs to sing?

What kind of music do you like to listen to?

What kind of dances do you like?

What is your favorite kind of food?

What kind of plants or flowers do you like?

What are ways in which you can help out around the house?

Share your answers on 🅕 Loving Lulu Stories

Dedication

This book is lovingly dedicated to all who may be experiencing a similar situation within their own family. My hope is that in sharing this story, it may offer some perspective for individuals and families on their journey with the elderly.

And to my two beauties, my mother Lucy and daughter Jessica, thank you for your love and for being my inspiration for this and so much more. I love you!

Glossary - Glosario

hello – hola
good bye – adiōs
friends – amigos
mother – madre
father – padre

loving – amorosa(o)
speak – hablar
cook – cocinar
food – comida
music – mūsica

grandmother – abuelita
grandfather – abuelito
grandparents – abuelitos
bienvenidos a mi mundo – welcome to my world
te quiero mucho – I love you very much
¿cōmo estās? – how are you?
 muy bien – very well

Loving Lulu

By Awilda Rivera Prignano

Illustrated by Lorraine Shulba

Sapphire Daisies
PRESS

Copyright #TXU002196544
Loving Lulu ISBN #978-1-7346520-2-4

Born and raised in the Windy City in the state commonly known as the Land of Lincoln, Awilda has always had a passion for writing and since childhood, dreamed of one day becoming a published writer. Her dream came true when she was published in the anthologies - Follow It Thru: Obstacles Equal Opportunities (June 2017), The Real Journey of the Empowered MomBoss (February 2018) and Your Shift Matters: Resistance to Resilience (November 2018). Besides writing, Awilda enjoys traveling and exploring new places. As a life-long learner, she will soon be embarking on an international adventure and will be living and working in different countries around the world. Awilda engages very easily with everyone she meets and her mission is to inspire through her storytelling, the values of love, kindness and compassion for others.

To learn more, please visit www.lovinglulu.com

Lorraine Shulba was born and raised in Alberta and began painting since she could hold a paintbrush. She has studied fine art at both Grant MacEwan University & the University of Alberta. Lorraine's work is in numerous public & private collections throughout Canada, the United States & England. She has been published in publications such as Prime-Time magazine, Synchronicity, See Magazine, & Scholastics Canada. She currently resides in Edmonton and can be seen skulking around coffee shops, sketch book in hand, waiting for inspiration. Lorraine loves commissions as well! Just ask! A professional graphic designer as well, she loves to help her clients get noticed!

Please visit her website www. lshulba.com
Design www.bluebugstudios.com